Water Features

for

Every Garden

Water Features for Every Garden

Helen Nash

Sterling Publishing Co., Inc.
New York

Acknowledgments

Every photo included in this book represents a cherished garden of the hospitable and sharing friends I encountered in my travels. While some photos were created by talented professionals—such as Bob BonGiorno in New York; Beau Royce, Larry Leon, and Brian Swensen in Dallas; Craig Luna in Atlanta; and C. Beaty Hanna and Chuck Thomas in Birmingham—most of them are the creative visions of their owners. I am grateful to the many water garden and koi clubs around the country that arranged most of my garden visits. It is the creativity of these backyard gardeners that inspires us to translate our dreams into our own gardens. Thank you all.

Library of Congress Cataloging-in-Publication Data
Nash, Helen, 1944–
    Water features for every garden / Helen Nash.
        p. cm.
    ISBN 0-8069-6096-5
    1. Water gardens. 2. Water in landscape architecture. I. Title.

SB423 .N378 2001
714—dc21   2001034851

10 9 8 7 6 5 4 3 2 1

Published by Sterling Publishing Company, Inc.
387 Park Avenue South, New York, N.Y. 10016
© 2001 by Helen Nash
Distributed in Canada by Sterling Publishing
℅ Canadian Manda Group, One Atlantic Avenue, Suite 105
Toronto, Ontario, Canada M6K 3E7
Distributed in Great Britain and Europe by Cassell PLC
Wellington House, 125 Strand, London WC2R 0BB, England
Distributed in Australia by Capricorn Link (Australia) Pty Ltd.
P.O. Box 704, Windsor, NSW 2756 Australia
Printed in Hong Kong
All rights reserved

Sterling ISBN 0-8069-6096-5

For Lyle Severson,
whose joyful spirit lives on in
every garden,
and for Jim Silzell,
who tends the
golden garden.

Contents

Introduction

WATER GARDENING
is the hottest gardening trend since the
vegetable garden. Even more remarkable is that the decision
to add water to our backyard landscapes coincides with a movement to
create backyard havens–a source of daily "vacations" from our hectic,
modern world. Just as our homes reflect our personalities and our
sense of design style, however eclectic, our gardens, too, give
play to such creative expression. Water and its inherent peace
and tranquility have a place in each of our garden designs. As you
explore these eighteen different garden styles and the water features to
include within them, invite your imagination to create your
own backyard living room, complete
with running water.

—HELEN NASH

CHAPTER ONE

The Formal Garden

*A formal Birmingham, Alabama, garden includes a rectangular, raised-edge
pond with side-spouting fountains and white tropical water lilies.*

Retaining Walls

Simplicity and restraint are the keys to a formal garden. Geometric shapes—circles, squares, rectangles, and ellipses, preferably laid out on a flat surface—symmetrically define the formal garden. Restraint in the number and colors of plants maintains the elegant design.

As with any garden design, first look to the design of the dominant structure—the home. A multistory, geometrically and symmetrically designed structure, often of brick or precisely cut stone, requests a formal garden, at least near the home itself. As the garden eases away from the formal home, its design can soften into curves and more informal layouts. Near the home, however, the garden is planned along a clear, central axis that is oriented to the house, with each individual part relating harmoniously to the whole.

In planning the formal garden, consider the shapes and their effect on the feeling of the garden: round and square shapes impose a feeling of rest and pause. Ellipses and rectangles create a sense of slow progression. Long, narrow shapes impose movement, almost an urgency to hurry through the area. For example, a large round or square open area, inviting pause, is the perfect place for garden seating and a show-case rose bed or pond. Long, elliptical or rectangular box-wood-hedged beds, divided by manicured pathways, invite

a leisurely walk to enjoy the garden scents. A narrow walkway, closely framed by tall hedges or vine-covered walls, hastens your passage.

Visual focal points lead the eye through the garden. While these may be statuary, planters, or garden structures, water features are particularly fitting. Along the narrow, enclosed pathway, picture a wall fountain. Along the wider garden pathway, envision

Elegant vertical blooms are suitable for a formal garden design.

flowing statues set within reservoir basins...and in the center of a large, open area, a reflecting pool with water lilies or a flowing fountain.

Home owners planning their own gardens are likely to take more liberties with a particular garden style than would a trained landscape architect. Whereas the professional landscape designer is likely to select symmetrically shaped plants, such as conical or columnar evergreens, the home owner may indulge a love of flowers. Judicious plant selection allows such leeway—delphinium, lupine, and foxglove supply vertical and formal accents. Cushion-forming low growers such as cushion mums work, too, as do tea roses, potted geraniums, and ferns. Avoid sprawling and irregularly shaped plants.

Within a water garden, water lilies suggest serene elegance, particularly if they are spaced to present calm reflections on the surface of the water. Reeds and rushes supply vertical elegance. Lush, large-leaved plants such as taro and canna are especially effective in corner plantings

A formally designed rectangular pool is a home to the elegant Victoria in this seaside garden.

or planters. Instant formality in pond design is achieved with raised geometric forms—either in the raised edge of the pond itself or in the raised bed in which the pond is installed, the pond design echoing that of the bed.

Retaining walls create raised planting beds and raised edges to garden ponds, primarily on level ground, although they are useful for terracing sloped sites, too. Because the main load-bearing pressure is exerted

sideways rather than downward, the foundation and the nature of the ground behind, below, and in front of the wall is critical. If the soil behind the wall is water-retentive, incorporate drainage provisions to prevent water buildup from adding extra weight at the rear and impairing the wall. A "toe" of foundation extending from the rear of the wall allows the weight of soil, and in the case of a pond, water, to help hold the whole structure in place. This foundation may need to be even deeper and thicker if

An elegant, formal Koi pond gains depth for the prize fish inside with a raised-wall design.

the soil directly in front of the wall is cultivated. Because foundations rely on the support of the soil surrounding them, build the foundation below the depth of cultivation.

The garden wall can be vertical, or you can "batter" it by sloping the wall gently backward to spread the center of gravity and add stability to the structure. Slope the wall one inch off the perpendicular for every foot of wall rise.

The stability of the retaining wall relies on the degree to which you can keep it dry at the rear. A layer of open drainage material behind the wall and a row of horizontal pipes (known as weep-holes) near the base provide the water drainage. Also, waterproofing the back of the wall with cement, plastic, or bitumen prevents water from passing through the wall itself and disfiguring it with lime salts or algae marks.

If you build the wall with concrete or mortar joining the stonework, include thermal movement joints, gaps of approximately 3/8 inches, to allow each panel to expand and contract independently. Likewise, thermal movement joints allow for initial shrinkage as the concrete sets in the newly built wall. Walls built of concrete blocks or reconstituted stone require joints at intervals equivalent to approximately two to two-

Classical statuary, such as this plumbed, stone statue of the Greek god Pan, becomes the focal point in a formal water garden.

The formal pool relies not only on geometric form but also on precisely cut and finished materials.

and-a-half times the height of the wall. Generally, thermal movement joints should not be more than 20 feet from a corner and no more than 40 feet apart in the main body of the wall. Brick walls need joints about every 10–12 feet.

Unless firm bedrock lies just below the surface of the soil, a good-quality concrete foundation or footing is necessary for mortar-bonded garden walls. The foundation must be substantial enough to prevent the structure from being affected by any subterranean movement. Its dimensions depend on the weight and thickness of the wall and the nature of the soil. It should also extend below the frost line for the area. Strip foundations are used for free-standing walls and for retaining walls, with the concrete extending to the rear to form a "toe."

Concrete for a strip foundation is laid in a flat-bottomed, vertically sided trench that follows the site of the proposed wall. Step the strip where the wall crosses contours of sloping ground. Make the strip twice as wide as the wall it will support. Build the wall along the center of the strip. Figure the depth of the strip by considering the soil type and the height and weight of the wall.

Stable soils need only a shallow foundation. For a 40-inch wall in gravelly soil over undisturbed, hard limestone, the concrete should be 1–2 feet deep. The same wall built on stiff, hard clay will need 2–3 feet of concrete. Unstable sand and flexible clays may require a foundation as deep or deeper than the height of the wall itself. If the frost level in the area is deeper than the depth required by the soil type, adjust the depth of the foundation to that point. For an enduring wall, ensure an adequate foundation.

A classic statue adds formal elegance to a shady pond.

A unique interpretation of a classic wall fountain uses a reservoir basin as the source of water piped to a shallow, overflowing basin at the top, from which the water flows down the face of the wall.

Water Features for Every Garden

A variation of the formal pool and flowing fountains is this narrow basin fed by a sheeting waterfall and spouting classic statuary.

In a formal garden setting, the pond design uses a raised and capped edge to frame its collection of aquatic plants.

Classic plant forms, classic urns, and a classic wall fountain fed from the small basin underneath complete a formal courtyard.

Formal design elements of a long, narrow rectangular pool below a stucco wall and wall fountain characterize an art deco design, popular in the 1920s.

A low brick-walled courtyard uses a raised, concrete-formed edge for a shallow water garden displaying a classic angel statue.

A preformed pond, carefully framed by limestone, creates a freestanding formal-style pool. The more precisely and smoothly cut the stone, the more formal the design.

A formal water feature commonly takes the form of a shallow pool with an elegant plumbed statue/fountain in its center.

Simple bell-fountain kits recycle water in a formal reflecting pool.

CHAPTER TWO

The Informal Garden

Informal pond designs are free-flowing, with the surrounding landscape complementing the pond form and materials.

Rock Edges for Garden Ponds

*M*OST *homes use an informal garden styling of curved and free-flowing lines. Usually, informal garden designs give primary consideration to the use of space. What will you do in any area of the personal landscape? Entertain family and friends? Provide a place for children to play? Supply the family with fresh vegetables and flowers? Enjoy a private escape from the world beyond? Informal gardens are most apt to meet these personal needs.*

Most aquatic plants, such as golden club (Orontium aquaticum), in the foreground, and water irises, work well in the informally designed pond.

Materials used in the informal garden echo those used in the home—wood, brick, stone. A brick ranch-style home, for example, could use less expensive pathways of bark chips with the paths themselves edged with design-compatible bricks.

Water features for informal gardens can include edging material that harmonizes with the home, especially if the water feature is constructed near the house. Flagstone paving used for walkways or patios can become a pond edge. Fortunately, the informal home is very rock-friendly. Whatever rock is used in the pond edging is easily carried out throughout the rest of the garden to aesthetically anchor the pond and/or stream within the landscape. However, when you select stone, consider its color compatibility with your home and existing structures. Stone, after all, comes in shades of blue, gray, black, brown, yellow, and red. Cobbles in the selected range allow the design scheme to extend throughout the garden with cobbles-to-pebbles used as actual groundcover or as design accents in small areas.

No doubt, the easiest way to install a garden pond is to

A shady garden echoes the free-form design of the pond in the adjacent deck, inviting quiet, relaxing time.

dig the hole, lay in the liner, and slap some rocks around the edge. If this works for you, so be it. However, if you want your pond to look like a real part of the surrounding land-scape, look at the basic rule for using rocks—rocks do not naturally sit upon the surface of the ground. In nature, rocks appear embedded within the earth. To achieve that same natural appearance with your pond, install the rock edging to appear embedded within its surroundings so that the water gently laps at the rocks. If the edging rock is too thin for this construction, double-stack the stone with one layer partially or wholly submerged and the upper layer above the water.

1. First make sure that the top level of your pond is perfectly level. Use a carpenter's level

or a water level to ascertain this.

2. Once the pond edge is established, excavate a shallow shelf one-half the depth of the thickness of the edging rocks. Be sure this shelf is also level all the way around the pond excavation.

3. Remember to slightly elevate the edge of the pond to prevent surface groundwater from washing into the pond.

4. Set in your liner, filling the pond nearly to the top to mold the liner to its excavated shell. Be sure enough excess liner extends beyond the coping or edging area, so you can dip it down and conceal it within the surrounding soil.

5. For stability, you may wish to set the edging rocks in a thin layer of mortar. If you use a double layer of rocks, complete the first round before adding the second, always checking the level as you work.

6. When the pond is filled, the water should lap up to the edge of the rocks set within the shallow shelf around the perimeter of the pond.

The center of an informal backyard is devoted to a slightly raised bed that includes a large double-pond design.

Near the Mississippi River, hilly terrain presents landscaping challenges. A level area claimed by the water garden is accessed by informal steps of railroad ties.

The use of planting pockets within the pond edging allows a change in color scheme with annual blooming plants.

A pond set off a deck becomes an integral part of the landscape by blending mature pond side plantings with the aquatics within.

Soil from the pond excavation creates a suitable mound for a waterfall in the informal design. Driftwood artistically complements the plantings and rockwork.

Pathways, streams, and ponds create a bird-friendly landscape in a suburban backyard.

Rounded rocks, many with interesting striations, are stacked to create a pleasing informal pond design.

Take advantage of the topsoil excavated from the pond to create a landscaping area around the waterfall. Blooming plants and ornamental grasses provide a delightful accent.

A very small area off the rear of a condominium home is landscaped informally with a waterfall and double-pond design. Rocks and flowers define the informal design.

Rough-hewn flagstone pavers form a low-maintenance walkway through a raised-bed design that incorporates both a stream and a pond.

Using a shallow pond-edge shelf, flat rocks are stacked from just below the water level to create a wide walkway around the pond.

A semi-formal, mortared-stone pond takes advantage of the sloping land to vary the pond edge with a higher retaining wall on its back edge. The Pennsylvania stone is also used as low-maintenance paving around the pond.

Loosely arranged rocks on the shallow edging shelf allow aquatic plants to scramble among them.

Larger stones, set on the shallow edging shelf, appear to emerge naturally from the water. If you plan to keep large Koi in the pond, select very smooth rocks. This will lessen the possibility of injury to these special pond pets.

CHAPTER THREE

Child-Safe Ponds

Donna Howard closely supervises Allison's time around the pond.

Pebble Ponds

ALTHOUGH *most insurance companies have yet to address ponds, legally ponds are "attractive nuisances," just like swimming pools. This means that if an uninvited child is injured in your pond, you are liable. Most insurance companies, however, consider a four-foot-high fence and a locked gate sufficient precaution to absolve you of liability. Beyond that is the consideration of local ordinances that govern construction. Those guidelines are for your protection, too. Listening to a builder who knows of ways to "get around" the rules is not in your best interest. That builder is likely to be long gone when a tragedy occurs in the pond that was built an inch short of local ordinances. A pond in your garden entices you to spend more time outside, so a fence provides more than legal protection. It gives you privacy and allows your backyard to be a genuine outside living area.*

Most insurance companies and local ordinances specify that gates to backyards containing "attractive nuisances," such as swimming pools and ponds, be kept locked.

Even though the pond is small and not even 24 inches deep, a solid fence keeps the pond safe from curious young children.

A brick wall and a sturdy gate provide privacy and safety to your garden.

one design element worthy of earmarking for immediate funds.

However, when young children are a part of the immediate family, the desire for the sound of flowing water and the yearning for the lush appeal of aquatic plants may seem a distant dream. You *can* have it all! Granted, water lilies may have to be grown in child-safe container gardens, but it's possible to have flowing water and the beauty of marginal aquatics safely in the presence of young children.

The solution is Jeff Salmon's "pebble pond." With an active two-year-old in the family, Jeff designed a shallow pond with a submersible pump to provide the sight and sound of moving water. Cobbles or rocks fill the pond *to the water's surface.* Any aquatic plant that doesn't require sur-face water for floating leaves can be planted in this pond. For that matter, even floating aquatics such as water hyacinth, water lettuce, water poppy, and floating heart still grow quite happily among the rocks of the pebble pond. Simply pull the rocks aside

A locked fence is a must if you include water in your garden design. Even if the water feature is less than a foot deep, for your own peace of mind be sure it is safe for your own family, as well as for friends, and perhaps even for people you don't know. Garden fencing allows you to create backdrops for the garden landscape, besides affording desirable privacy. In a world of stress and con-crete, knowing that you have a built-in retreat of peace, tranquility, and privacy at home may mean more than a brief vacation. A decorative fence, perhaps covered with lush vines or partially con-cealed by shrubs and trees, is and insert the potted plants. Think of this type of pond as a compromise—it provides most of the desirable pond elements while still being fully child-safe. The pebble pond can be built above ground or in ground, and it can be any size desired.

The depth of a pebble pond need accommodate only the submersible pump and allow for any plant pots to be concealed by rocks. If you plan to eventually convert the pebble pond to a rock-free water garden that includes water lilies and goldfish, make the depth 18 to 24 inches and use a base filling beneath the cobbles. Used plant containers work well.

With the Koi pond set away from the house, the Kinneys use a wrought-iron fence with a locked gate to protect both children and fish.

A variation on the brick wall is a lattice construction that allows light to pass through.

A stockade fence is a relatively inexpensive fencing option that is easily camouflaged with perimeter plantings.

A high fence around the pond creates a private outdoor living room.

A small, shallow container is filled with potted aquatic plants. Selected stones fill in gaps between the plants and afford a decorative touch. A small bubbling pump enhances the mini-garden with the sight and sound of moving water.

Mature plantings all but fully hide the privacy fence around the Cannons' backyard so that they can enjoy their time outdoors with their special Koi.

The "pebble-pond" may be constructed above- or in-ground. A submersible pump equipped with a foaming fountain head provides the sight and sound of moving water. Rocks completely fill the pond to the water surface. Potted aquatic plants, as desired, are set among the rocks.

The "pebble-pond" may be as small as you like. Select your stones to coordinate with the rest of your garden landscape.

CHAPTER FOUR

The Rock Garden

Reseeding Johnny-jump-ups scramble among the rocks surrounding the pond edge. A dwarf conifer anchors the scene in the winter landscape.

Rocks in Ponds

*I*T *used to be that rock gardens needed gritty soil and sharp drainage to grow alpine plants in traditional low-maintenance schemes. Do-it-yourself gardeners have changed all that. Since rocks are an important part of land-scaping design, and low-maintenance is a major concern of busy gardeners, combining rock-garden designs with regular garden plants–annuals, perennials, ornamental grasses, and shrubs–offers a welcome option in garden design. Including rock-edged water gardens ensures the popularity of the idea.*

Part of the fun of using rocks in the garden are weekend "collecting" trips to find just the right rock for the waterfall or surrounding landscape.

Key design elements of the rock garden remain. Low-growing or specimen plants interspersed with rocks and open ground prevail. Open ground is covered with low-maintenance materials such as bark-mulch or small gravel. There the similarities end: no more concern if the climate is appropriate for contrary alpines; no more worry about drainage for temperamental plants. Instead, we indulge ourselves with annuals, perennials, dwarf conifers, whatever plants befit the land-scaping scheme. They are simply set among rocks.

The new rock garden is especially suited for land-scaping the water garden. Ponds are edged with rocks. The rocks extend out into the surrounding area to visually anchor the pond creation within the landscape. It is then a simple matter of selecting plants of appropriate size, shape, and color to fit the landscape scheme. But what about including rocks within the pond itself?

A primary attraction of water features is that water "naturalizes" the garden. Although we can make water features look quite natural, we are *not* recreating nature. Clear water features found in nature are open systems, with nature providing natural ways of cleansing and replenishing the water. Our artificial, backyard creations are closed systems, much like indoor aquariums, requiring aid in cleansing and replenishing.

Using rocks within a backyard pond is certainly possible, but it does create more work/maintenance for the pond that is also home to fish. Organic sediment, ranging from decomposing plant parts to fish feces, naturally collects between rocks, under them, and on the bottom of the pond. In the low-oxygen environment down in the rocks, anaerobic bacteria work to decompose the organic matter. Their by-product is deadly, fish-toxic hydrogen sulfide, which also makes the pond water smell bad. To protect your fish, and to prevent a foul-smelling pond, annually draining the pond and thoroughly cleaning the debris underneath and between the rocks is necessary. If you don't mind this labor-intensive maintenance—usually performed when the water is chilled in the autumn—or if you can afford to hire someone to do the job, lining your pond with rocks can be quite attractive. Bear in mind, however, that algae quickly cover the rocks,

A true rock garden is like this scree garden: rocks and coarse gravel accented with hardy plants that endure the extremes of temperature characteristic of high elevations.

and bacteria work to decompose any organic matter settling onto the rocks. The bacterial activity stains the rocks bluish-black, which will very likely detract from your aesthetic intentions and plea-

sure. An artistic compromise would be to use rocks within the pond only in special areas, such as on a shallow planting shelf or within a shallow bog area. This option precludes the need to drain the pond

 Water Features for Every Garden

Where craggy rocks are commonly found, flat specimens make excellent pond edges.

for cleaning since the cobbles can be removed manually and a pond vac used to clean the small area.

Using rocks in a running-stream design, however, is more successful; the flowing water helps clean the rocks, even as it provides oxygenated water to hasten aerobic bacterial reduction of organic sediment. To ensure a low-maintenance stream, mortar the base rocks of the stream onto the liner. Besides preventing sediment from collecting down in the rocks, this also promotes the water running over, rather than under, the rocks.

Even though the new rock garden uses traditional annuals and perennials, you can still use rock-garden-style plantings, such as small plants tucked among the rocks.

Smooth pea gravel, available in various color tones, makes a good filler between larger rocks. Showcased with selected cobbles are artistic rock creations.

The rocks selected for the backyard landscape are usually those commonly found in the area.

A new pond construction with rocks on the pond bottom is quite beautiful.

However, in a short time, algae and bacterial decomposition discolor the underwater rocks and produce a black, foul-smelling sludge.

Fish kept in a rock-bottomed pond are at risk from toxic hydrogen sulfide produced by anaerobic bacteria-decomposing organic matter among the rocks. Your nose warns you this is happening, as does a white fish displaying stress-indicative pink blushing in fins, tail, and body. These fish need help in a hurry, and the pond needs a thorough cleaning.

CHAPTER FIVE

The Tropical/Rainforest Garden

Tropical or rainforest ponds are characterized by lush plantings. The texture of those plantings, such as ferns and palms, further defines the garden style.

Vegetable Filters

LUSH *describes the tropical/rainforest garden–lots of large, green leaves; lots of brightly colored flowers; lots of texture contrast with finely dissected foliage. Typical of Zone 10 or Florida gardens, the tropical garden is reminiscent of rainforests of orchids and exotic flowers. All these tropical plants, however, can be grown in northern gardens in containers. Have wheels, will travel! Mandevillea? No problem. Bouganvillea? No problem. Taro? No problem. It doesn't matter where your garden grows, it can be graced with tropical plants.*

Tropical water lilies, traditionally held high above the water surface, lend tropical ambiance to the pond.

Within the pond, few plants can match the extravagance of canna blooms and foliage.

Interestingly, northern gardens do not need tropical plants for a tropical/rainforest look. The essence of a lush, tropical-looking garden is abundance. Grow lots of plants. Plant them close together. Provide large-leaved specimens. Contrast their boldness with delicate, lacy forms such as ferns and fern-leafed specimens. Include large-flowered specimens such as canna and hardy hibiscus. Try some of the new plant introductions, such as the hardy banana that dies back to the ground each year but still produces five feet or more growth each season.

Groundcover plants enhance the tropical garden, too. Temperate gardens can indulge in hardy groundcovers and then

---

tuck in potted tropicals, such as bromeliads. Within the water garden, any tropical plant may be grown in any climate zone. In temperate zones, move them outdoors only after the water temperature has warmed to 70 degrees F. In the autumn, as the days shorten and the temperatures cool, move the plants indoors for warmth and supplemental lighting.

Certain tropical aquatic plants, such as umbrella palm, papyrus (both miniature and giant forms), and taro can be grown within the pond or planted in self-contained pond-pots that can be set anywhere in the garden. While you are selecting tropical specimens for your rainforest garden, be sure to include the floating tropicals, water

The ambiance of tropical design is enhanced by contrasts in color-dark against light; variegations against solids; color, blues, and grays against green.

hyacinth, water lettuce, and Neptunia. Parrot's feather, while a temperate-zone plant, lends lush tropical feel to the water. Even as abundant plants fill the pond, they also work to keep the pond water crystal clear.

So long as you ensure that the fish load in your pond does not approach or exceed the maximum stocking capacity of the pond (generally one inch of goldfish or

one-half inch of Koi per square foot of exposed water surface), vegetable filtration can keep your water clear and safe. Vegetable filtration uses aquatic plants to remove excess nutrients from the pond water. Allowing water to flow through the roots of these plants also produces mechanical filtration as fine, suspended particulate matter is collected by exposed plant roots. The incidence of floating hyacinth roots is a case in point. By removing the plants and applying a strong hosing to the roots, the particulate matter is cleansed and the plants again resume normal immersion of roots.

Bio-filters installed at the top of a waterfall benefit from the extra boost of vegetable filtration, usually supplied by floating water hyacinth or hydroponically grown water celery *(Oenanthe)* or watercress *(Nasturtium officinale)*. These plants perform the same function tucked among rocks in the waterfall or a stream.

If you construct a vegetable-filter pond, size it to at least ten percent of the area of your main pond. A vegetable-filter pond need not be as deep as your main pond since most of the plants used will be either submerged aquatic plants, free-floaters, or shallow-water marginals. Recycle the water from the main or reservoir pond to the top or back of the vegetable pond. As the water flows through that pond on its way back to the main pond, nutrients are removed, bio-filtration proceeds, and some mechanical filtration occurs. This double-pond concept lends itself to interesting designs, including stream constructions as vegetable filters. It is also a way to keep mischievous Koi away from tender aquatic plants.

Tropical taro, available in greens, variegations, and red-to-black leaves, is a staple in the tropical pond.

Lush, lush, lush, and color, color, color define the tropical look.

A tropical garden includes tropical plants, lavish color, and abundant plantings.

Contrasts in texture create a tropical mood.

Pendulous Datura injects a classic tropical form above the lush growth of aquatic plants.

A potted palm on wheels lends instant tropical flavor to the garden.

Begonias and bromeliads provide tropical accent in the summer garden and brighten indoor wintry days for Northerners.

A waterfall framed by taro and palm? Pure tropical.

A temperate Oklahoma pond gains a tropical feeling with the use of taro and parrot's feather in the pond.

Water hyacinth and parrot's feather are functional, tropical treatments for the top of a bio-filter, aiding in the removal of excess nutrients from the pond water.

Umbrella palm
within the pond
easily substitutes
for palm foliage.

Garden texture is amplified by subtle color even among the green shades.

Astilbe, daylilies, and water lilies add color to this pond landscape. In the bio-filter at the top of the waterfall, water celery grows hydroponically for vegetable filtration, with lush ambiance.

Enhance the function of bio-filters made from heavy-duty stock tanks with aquatic plants in the top. Note the size of these water hyacinths, happily fed by water nutrients.

Water celery (Oenanthe) grows vigorously in the bio-filter unit of the waterfall and in its courseway, keeping the pond water clear.

CHAPTER SIX

The Collector's Garden

*Plant collectors appreciate the garden enhancement of
ponds and other water features.*

Koi, Plants, and Pocket Bogs

*A*VID *gardeners fall in love with plants. Often these love affairs involve a particular plant family–roses, hostas, ferns, begonias. Frequently, these collecting gardeners discover the attraction of including water features among their cherished plants. Besides the pleasing sight and sound of moving water, a special plant is doubly appreciated when reflected in pristine water.*

A preformed pond, set above ground level to prevent groundwater from contaminating the pool, uses a double layer of rounded rocks to create a planting bed around it.

In my travels, I have been captivated by the water gardens designed by plant collectors. Among the most special have been shady pond and stream gardens lovingly framed with very special hostas. Garden pathways are an important design element in these collectors' gardens. Often these paths open up to cozy areas where both plants and water can be savored.

Plant collectors, being plant lovers, often fall prey to affection for aquatic plants. Many water gardeners have filled their gardens with pool after pool to display an ever-growing collection of water lilies. Interestingly, many plant collectors become Koi collectors, as well. A Koi pond devoid of plants allows the fullest enjoyment of these special fish, as well as providing the perfect foil for surrounding plant collections.

For the Koi keeper, combining Koi and aquatic plants can be frustrating. First of all, Koi are not goldfish. Averaging three times the size of a mature goldfish, a Koi has amplified levels of needs—more oxygen in the water, more depth in which to live,

Dramatic plant combinations showcase special plants.

Framing the waterfall of a stream, hosta appreciates the proximity of water.

and more space in which to swim. A Koi pond includes certain features: a minimum depth of three feet, preferably more; well-oxygenated water, often enhanced with venturi or air-jet systems; excellent, highly effective filtration systems, often including bottom drains, to provide both clear and chemically safe water; protection from predators and harsh sunlight; no shallow shelves that provide launching pads for predators; no gravel on the pond bottom; and no sharp objects within the pond itself.

In looking at aquatic plants in their natural habitat, notice that they grow in the shallows around the edge of the water. Even water lilies grow in only 2 to 3 feet of water. Since Koi need a minimum depth that is the maximum depth for plants, pedestals or other means of propping up plants to their optimum depth are necessary.

Often water gardens are designed to recreate nature. Stone is extended into the edge of the water, and many water gardens use stone on the pond bottom. Besides the physical threat of injury, stone used within a pond creates a serious health threat to Koi, as toxic hydrogen sulfide is produced by bacterial decomposition of organic debris among the rocks. Hidden accumulations of sediment among rocks also provide a haven for disease-bearing bacteria and parasites that might harm your Koi. Healthy conditions in a dedicated Koi pond require a clean pond.

Surface-covering plants, such as water lilies and water hyacinths, inhibit oxygen uptake of the water. Ordinarily, the primary source of oxygen in the pond water is at the water surface. Supplemental aeration may be necessary even with low fish-stocking levels. However, water lilies are a calm-water plant, not happy at all growing in moving, choppy, or sprayed water.

Yet another conflict between Koi and plants lies in the nature of the beasts. Koi are grazers, enjoying salad or greens. Tender aquatic plants become part of the food chain. Submerged grasses may never survive with large Koi. Floating plants quickly die, as their roots are nibbled away. Often, large Koi noses uproot water lilies and other aquatic plants in their quest for tasty morsels. A heavily planted pond also compro-

mises oxygen levels—during the daytime plants give off oxygen in photosynthesis, but at night they take up oxygen in respiration.

Especially if you have invested money in your Koi collection, you'll want to shade their pond to protect their colors. Shadecloth setups are relatively inexpensive options in design, although many Koi ponds are designed with decorative pergolas and lattice roofs. Since

most aquatic plants require six hours or more of sunlight each day, aquatic plant options are limited with this pond design.

Because Koi are enjoyed most for their color, patterns, and size, new hobbyists begin collecting them for just those reasons. Yet, a well-planted water garden conceals the fish even as the design requirements for each differ. With all these conflicts, serious Koi and aquatic-plant collectors keep

A dedicated Koi pond supplies ideal conditions for a collection of special fish, just as the surrounding landscape supplies ideal conditions for special plants.

their treasures in separate quarters, but they can be kept together with a pocket-bog design.

Easily created with the initial excavation, a bog pocket is simply a shallow shelf dug out in the pond edge. Once the liner is in place, select large rocks to frame the bog pocket and then fill it in with smaller cobbles. With framing rocks close to the water surface, large fish are discouraged from entering the area while small fish enjoy a quiet haven.

To ease maintenance of both the pond and the pocket plants, keep the plants within containers. If planted directly in the cobbles, happy aquatic plants send their roots throughout. Eventually, they need thinning and division. Lifting a pot is easier than sorting through a tangle of rocks, plants, and roots.

A pocket bog is simply a shallow shelf created at the edge of the pond. Lined with attractive cobblestones, the bog collection of aquatic plants is kept safe from the resident Koi.

Unsuspecting Koi keepers are surprised at the devastation the large fish inflict upon water lilies and other aquatic plants.

A solution to keeping Koi and plants? Keep them separated.

While Koi and aquatic plants can be kept separated with a bog area apart from the main pond, such as this bog between the waterfall and the Koi pond, plant selections are necessarily limited.

Another way to collect both Koi and aquatic plants is to confine water lilies to shallow areas around the edge of the pond.

Dwarf Acorus gramineus 'Ogon,' a yellow-foliaged plant, combines well with dwarf lotus in a side-pocket planting.

Create a shallow shelf in the initial construction and build a separating wall with large rocks. In this pond, the bog area is filled with soil that is kept wet by water seeping through the rock divider.

Although lotuses bloom in August, their foliage adds a dramatic presence in pocket bogs or within their own container ponds.

Keeping bog-pocket plantings confined within their own pots makes for easier maintenance.

CHAPTER SEVEN

The Cottage Garden

The cottage garden is synonymous with an array of blooming flowers. Water is a natural complement.

Eclectic Flowers and Water

THE cottage garden tradition began in country gardens with utilitarian plantings of vegetables and herbs and with ponds built for livestock. Any remaining space was filled in with whatever flowering perennials and native plants the lady of the house enjoyed or was given. Over time, the cottage garden style became synonymous with a tumble of flowering plants—vines cascading over arbors and fences, and a succession of flowering perennials, rarely in planned color schemes—flowers for drying, flowers for cutting, flowers for scent, and flowers for color, all in free-flowing beds, indulging their spread and reseeding.

style, the abundance of flowers establishes the design. Winding pathways among the flower beds, framed with spilling plants, make the garden a romantic adventure. Garden structures become important elements of the garden design: clematis and rose-covered arbors, wisteria-draped pergolas, container-laden decks and lanais, and gazebos framed by graceful pampas grass or whispering miscanthus and bedecked with hanging baskets of

A water garden within a cottage garden is not complete without water lilies and their continuous display of flowers throughout the summer and into fall.

Modern renditions of the cottage garden are found in planned urban developments where developers plant common and inexpensive juniper, taxus, burning bush, nandina, and youpon. Rather than yank out the base plantings of the new home, home owners "dress them up" by tucking in perennials and ornamental grasses. While the presence of the basic shrubs and the addition of popular ornamental grasses are not traditionally in the cottage asparagus fern, trailing petunias, and scented geraniums.

Stream gardens, flowing fountains, birdbaths, tub gardens, Koi ponds, and a water garden overflowing with lush aquatic plants readily complement the new cottage garden style. While stone is used to edge the pond and stream, it is secondary to the plantings brought to the edge of water features and blended with the aquatic plants within. The new cottage garden has evolved into an eclectic indulgence of life and color!

Lush water hyacinths merge with pond-edge plantings of perennial verbena.

Low-maintenance decking and a pergola shelter a semi-shaded flower garden embracing a stream and water garden.

Granny Green's Ohio cottage garden features a concrete pond in the center. All paths through the glorious flowers meet at the fully planted water garden.

The modern-day cottage garden offers eclectic combinations in lieu of traditional herbs, vegetables, and flowers: an ephemeral smoke tree joins elegant daylilies and other perennials around the free-form pond.

What cottage garden is complete without supplying water to the birds attracted by the potpourri of flowers?

Ornamental grasses add yet another dimension to the cottage style. Beside this shady pond, variegated ribbon grass (Phalaris 'Picta') combines with New Guinea impatiens for light and color.

A stream set among flowering Rose of Sharon and perennials empties into a lushly planted water garden graced with several 'Pink Perfection' hardy water lilies.

An island bed features a water garden.

What cottage-style spring-time Northern garden is complete without redbuds in bloom and the first flush of azaleas?

Perennial selections around a pond provide a season-long succession of color.

CHAPTER EIGHT

The Bird, Butterfly, and Wildlife Garden

*A bird- and butterfly-friendly garden offers native and cultivated
plants attractive to garden visitors.*

Bird Ponds

As the modern world of concrete encroaches on us, our private gardens become critical havens of food, shelter, and water for wildlife. Although birds and butterflies most immediately come to mind, other lives in nature need and appreciate the havens we create outside the back door—squirrels, rabbits, dragonflies, beneficial insects, turtles, even bats. In creating a wildlife garden, consider combinations of plants that will sustain those lives. It's not enough to plant a flower attractive to a butterfly; you must also include feeding plants for the less-appealing butterfly larvae, the caterpillars.

Wildlife gardens are conceived three-dimensionally: the floor of the garden, the mid-level, and the higher level among treetops. They offer both open areas and the safety of thickets. Creating such a garden requires research. Find out what wildlife is native to your area, and then determine what habitat and feeding requirements they need throughout the year. Native plants are a major component in the wildlife garden. Your state's department of natural resources and your local county extension office are most helpful with this research. The National Wildlife Federation offers comprehensive information through its offices, website, and Backyard Habitat program.

Water is essential to wildlife. The garden pond or stream is a welcome addition to the wildlife garden. Because birds carry parasites that may infect your fish, you may decide to create a separate water feature for birds. Birds need to know that the water is shallow enough for their wading and bathing. Pea gravel on the bottom of the water feature helps them see that the water depth is safe.

A water feature attractive to birds includes access to the water. A shallow beach area, stones that emerge from the water, or driftwood emerging from the pool provides access and perching. Keep the water source open enough to let the birds feel safe from predators. If plantings frame the feature, at least one side should be kept in low plantings. A shrub or small tree offers preening sojourns after the refreshing bath.

Steve Katona designed a bird pond that was featured in Helen Nash's *Pond & Garden* magazine (May/June 2000). Built into slightly sloped ground, the shallow excavation offers many channels and pools of water that flow from the uppermost entry pool. Stone is mortared over

Pet waterfowl enjoy a reservoir-fed system that allows water to drip into a shallow basin that overflows into the cobbles covering the reservoir below.

the entire liner with careful attention to water access. Water throughout the feature is kept very shallow, at no more than three inches deep, so that the entire pool is bird-accessible. At the base of the pool, the water flows into a hidden reservoir. The whiskey barrel container, covered by a grate and camouflaged with rocks, holds the submersible pump that cycles the water through the system.

Within your own water garden, include plants attrac-

Water gardens become bird-friendly when you supply access to the water. Rocks protruding above the shallow water or at the edge of the pond and pieces of drift-wood for perching are engraved invitations.

tive to birds and insects. Cardinal flower, for example, is a hummingbird magnet. Watercress grown in a waterfall attracts insects, and the insects

Dragonflies and damselflies patrol the pond and garden perimeters, feeding on smaller insects.

and water attract birds. Cattails, left in place through the winter, offer hibernation quarters to insects that feed early returning red-wing blackbirds in the spring. During the winter, keeping a hole open in the ice in the pond may offer your favorite pair of cardinals and their friends the only available water in

the neighborhood.

Creating a wildlife garden can evolve unsuspectingly. Often it happens after the installation of the first water garden. Suddenly dragonflies and birds never seen before appear in the garden. Small decisions of including a plant attractive to wildlife only hint at the commitment to come. Once we realize how closely interrelated all of nature is, including our urban backyards, garden design becomes a very personal passion.

Chleome, *turtle head, growing in damp soil, attracts birds, butterflies, and pollinating bees.*

Butterflies are so attracted to the tropical, aquatic Gymnocoronis that the common name of the plant is "butterfly plant." The delectable, white pompon blooms appear at just the right time to feed hungry butterflies.

An early-season lotus bed provides cover for a mother wood duck and her brood. Can you find adventurous "Waldo" among the lotus leaves?

Cardinal flower, Lobelia cardinalis, *blooms in summer within the pond shallows to attract hummingbirds to the garden.*

A wildlife pond can be planned to include waterfowl, too. Within this large farm pond is a special ramped duck-house. Although including waterfowl in a pond often leads to green water, the joy of keeping ducks takes precedence.

If you build a pond, the birds will come.

Set up with a waterfall to recycle the pond water, this mud-bottom pond displays the first intrusion of a common problem to the natural wildlife pond--cattails. To control the wildlife-attractive cattails, wade out into the cold autumn waters--wearing waders, of course--and cut the cattails back below the water level.

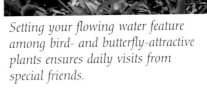

Setting your flowing water feature among bird- and butterfly-attractive plants ensures daily visits from special friends.

CHAPTER NINE

The Deck Garden

The deck garden does not have to be attached to your home. The Donnellys in Missouri created an island deck garden within their immediate backyard.

Wheelchair-Accessible Ponds

A DECK *addition meets lifestyle demands for an area close to the home for family entertaining. Often decks are embellished with potted plants framing entries, accenting corners, and decorating entertainment areas.*

A simple deck off the back of the home becomes very special with a pond set nearby and comfortable seating positioned to enjoy the life in the water.

Since much time is spent outside, plan to include a water feature either near or on the deck. Enclose a preformed pond within a decorative frame set upon the deck itself, or install one within the deck construction. An in-deck pond is best constructed with the initial deck construction so that adequate support can be brought up to the edge of the pond. The pond can be as simple as a small water garden and goldfish pond, or it can be as elaborate as a fully equipped Koi pond.

Another type of deck pond is the pond built just off the side of the deck. These ponds may be in-ground or they may be built upon the ground. Their close proximity to the family living area allows for frequent enjoyment.

Deck ponds can exist elsewhere within the garden, too. Just as paved areas or decks are installed around swimming pools, so, too, can they be used as low-maintenance and accessible surrounds for a water garden. A deck pond becomes the center of an entertainment or private relaxation area. Maintenance is as simple as a whisk of a broom.

The deck pond offers critical accessibility for the handicapped, as well. Board-walks through the garden and around the pond allow wheelchairs to venture into the garden. A raised pond with deck access even allows the wheelchair-bound to work within the pond, pruning away dying foliage or fertilizing plants.

Josh Spece, who was born with a form of muscular dys-trophy, shared his wheelchair-acces-sible pond with *Pond & Garden* readers (Jan/Feb 2001). Josh's family built their large water garden into a sloped area of their Iowa yard. Three sides of the pond are surrounded by soil and landscape plantings. The fourth side, however, is built as a wall with 2 x 4 and 2 x 6 lumber sup-port. The narrow side allows Josh to reach into the chair-high pond and work with his plants and fish. The Speces even took advantage of the structure to include a shady pergola. Josh noted that the entire pond could be built as a raised structure to allow access all around.

Perhaps the most wheelchair-accessible ponds, Josh notes, are container or tub gardens. Whether displaying a collec-tion of aquatic plants or a single, large specimen, whiskey-barrel-size containers are just the right height for tending from a chair. Including several on the easily acces-sible deck makes for attrac-tive, easily tended displays.

Decks make for easy maintenance. Container plants provide color and a touch of green. Building a pond off the deck creates the delightful illusion of waterside living.

Two sides of this Koi pond are framed with zigzag decking to provide a low-maintenance family living area.

Including a Koi pond within the decking adjacent to family living areas allows frequent enjoyment of these special finned pets.

Various elevations of decking throughout the yard create both pond and low-maintenance planting areas.

Even a small urban lot affords enough room for a Koi pond and an entertainment deck.

Small planting beds next to the deck allow landscaping to frame the deck pond.

Bob BonGiorno of Dix Hills, New York, designed a very special garden with Japanese detail. Attractive wooden decking provides safe garden pathways.

Undaunted by an unfortunate accident, musician Dwight Carson gains access to and enjoyment of his Koi pond and garden with wheelchair-friendly decking and pathways.

In Atlanta, Craig Luna used decking as garden pathways that also form a bridge over the stream and water garden.

In-deck ponds perform two services: they allow the inclusion of a pond within a limited space, and they bring the water garden or Koi pond within the immediate living area.

The Hunters' Louisville garden uniquely includes a large display garden for her prize-winning roses and a decked Koi pond for his prize-winning Koi. Guess where the Hunters spend most of their time.

Constructing an In-Deck Pond

Ideally, the in-deck pond is constructed with the initial deck construction. This allows support to be built right up to the edge of the pond.
Photo by Greg Maxwell

Customize the deck construction to fit a preformed pond unit or build it for lining with a pond membrane, as shown here.
Photo by Greg Maxwell

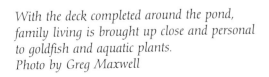

With the deck completed around the pond, family living is brought up close and personal to goldfish and aquatic plants.
Photo by Greg Maxwell

Water Features for Every Garden

CHAPTER TEN

The Patio/Courtyard Garden

Typically, the courtyard garden features a paved center with perimeter planting beds. Tucking a water garden into a perimeter bed enhances the garden.

Container Gardens

You don't need to live in a condominium to create a patio or courtyard garden. A paved area off the back of a home or within a center atrium, enclosed within walls, creates the setting. Typically these areas focus on entertainment with garden plantings as decorative accents. The plantings may be formal or informal, depending on the style of the home and its courtyard. Water features, such as wall fountains, plumbed statuary set within a basin or fed by a reservoir (hidden or visible), or small ponds set within perimeter areas add life and sparkle to the cozy area. Because of space limitations, container gardens are most commonly used.

Whiskey-barrel-size containers and flatter dish gardens can support a complete mini-water garden: a water lily, two or three shallow-water aquatic plants, a few goldfish, some submerged grasses, and even an ornament or feature that recycles water from the container. Tub gardens serve also to display aquatic specimens such as lotus, taro, Thalia, or giant papyrus. Since any watertight container can be used to display aquatic plants, including aquatic plants in courtyard décor expands the design possibilities of these small gardens.

A courtyard accessed through French doors is defined by a low brick wall. Within the perimeter bed, a raised formal pond features aquatic plants, water ornaments, and a cherub statue.

Wall fountains are perfect for the courtyard garden. Usually equipped with their own shallow reservoir and a small submersible pump to direct the water via a plastic tube to the top of the feature, these small fountains may simply flow from a spigot.

A classically designed wall fountain befits the more formally designed courtyard. The water reservoir and its submersible pump are concealed within or behind the wall.

A shallow marsh pond with a plumbed statue is the centerpiece of the courtyard.

This classic wall-fountain design cycles water from the small pond down below. Because water naturally draws back unless the water force is strong enough, prevent a wet wall by increasing the capacity of the pump or by shortening the distance the water falls.

A freestanding, flat-backed fountain feature appears to be a wall fountain.

A small overflowing fountain brightens a shady nook in the courtyard garden.

Small water features need not include aquatic plants. A small pump, set among a collection of rocks bubbles vigorously.

A narrow courtyard garden features a concrete stream winding through the perimeter beds to connect two ponds at opposite ends of the wraparound garden.

Although courtyard walls are usually constructed of solid materials, a brick lattice design allows light to penetrate the privacy wall.

CHAPTER ELEVEN

The Xeriscaped Garden

The xeriscaped garden includes plants that do not require frequent watering. Often these plants bear water-conserving foliage that is small, hairy, needle-thin, thick and fleshy, and blue-green to silvery-white.

Reservoir Water Features

DRY summer regions and heavily populated areas that rely on municipally supplied water benefit from the xeriscaped garden design. These gardens make use of plants that do not require frequent watering. Plants that survive in low-water conditions often have hairy leaves, lower-chlorophyll content reflected by blue-gray to silver color, and needle-thin or thick, fleshy foliage to better conserve water. Often native plants in an area enter into this category, especially if the climate is dry. Spaces between plantings are covered with low-maintenance and water-conserving layers of stone or bark mulch.

perature control of the water. Holding twice the volume of water used by the visible feature, the reservoir is equipped with a submersible pump that directs water through a plastic tube to the feature above. For

In Las Vegas, Nevada, gardens make use of attractive stone groundcover and framed beds to display water-conservative plants.

Surprisingly, a water garden is one of the most water-conserving of garden features, with less evaporation and topping off compared to traditional watering of landscape and lawn. Designing a water feature with a hidden reservoir takes fullest advantage of this, especially if the feature does not include a fountain spray that increases evaporation.

Hidden reservoirs are constructed in the ground where they gain insulation and temperature control of the water. a simple overflowing water feature, size the pump by figuring 1.5 times the height from the pump to the top of the feature. Find the cut-off column on the manufacturer's pump chart and follow its directives for that height.

The reservoir itself is simply a watertight container

A xeriscaped stream uses rock décor rather than plants. Cobbled spillways and elevation changes result in less evaporation.

Studies show that a water garden uses less water than that required with a traditional lawn and garden.

A pond in the xeriscaped landscape is a refreshing oasis.

holding the requisite volume of water. Often whiskey-barrel liners, holding 80 gallons of water, are sufficient for small overflowing features. However, when necessary, a large enough hole can be lined with pond membrane to provide water volume. A heavy-duty plastic or fiberglass grate is fitted over the top of the reservoir and covered with cobblestones. With the water feature set in the center of the cobbles and the plastic tubing connected to the outflow valve of the pump inconspicuously brought up to the top of the feature, the pump is plugged in and the water flows, overflowing through the cobbles and back into the hidden reservoir. Reservoir-fed water features can take many forms: an overflowing millstone, a trickling wall fountain, an overflowing container garden, a shallow bird pond, or even a two-foot-deep water garden. Just be certain that the reservoir is wide enough to accept all the overflowing water!

Cacti, of course, are superb plantings for hot, dry conditions. Northern gardens gain the same effect with a planting of prickly pear.

A large pond and specimen plantings protected by water-conserving mulch define this Dallas backyard.

Take advantage of all parts of the water display to include flowers. This stream supports a water poppy (Hydrocleys) and its delicate yellow blooms.

In an arid garden, the most lavish blooms may be on your tropical water lilies, such as this N. 'Emily Grant Hutchings.'

Many regions of the country experience dry summers. Providing water-retentive ground cover and selective planting of drought-friendly plants, such as sedums, still allows creative landscaping in dry conditions.

In spite of dry conditions, a water garden can display the most lush of tropical plants.

Sedum 'John Creech' blankets one side of a Midwestern garden, barely acknowledging rain-free summers.

Supply two to two-and-a-half times the amount of water required by the water feature within a hidden reservoir below the overflowing feature. For a simple feature, such as this millstone set in the center of a wide garden path, a whiskey-barrel container is more than adequate. The sight is so unexpected, you cannot help but kneel and touch the strangely reflective surface!

Specimen drought-friendly plantings frame a unique water display on the edge of the pond.

A protected wall fountain and its basin pond are protected from water-evaporative winds.

Set up a small submersible pump in the bottom of your hidden reservoir, and use a grate to cover the top. Cobblestones conceal the grate. For an enchanting display, pick a spouting ornamental statue, connect it to your submerged pump, and plant either aquatic or moisture-loving plants among the cobbles. Here the little girl "waters" water forget-me-nots (Myosotis aquatica) that produce charming blue blooms through much of the summer.

The Japanese Garden

Key elements of a Japanese garden are stone, green plants, and water.
The Japanese statue is enhanced by these basic elements.

Stepping Stones and Zigzag Bridges

*F*OR centuries, the Japanese garden style has been revered as an artistic creation and as an embodiment of a philosophy honoring nature and the inner spirit of life. Even without understanding the symbolism of its elements, garden visitors are captivated by the serenity of green colors, the living artistry of precisely pruned trees and shrubs, the aesthetics of stone lanterns, bamboo, and rocks, as well as by the mystery of the garden path and the magic of water.

While flowers are allowed in the Japanese garden, they play a limited role among the predominantly green plantings set among natural stone.

Although very specific guidelines require years of study, you can create your own Japanese garden. However, planning your Japanese garden is more than simply supplying a stone lantern or a deer scare. First you must create the basic garden. It demands a certain restraint to forget your grandmother's phlox and her petunias. Flowers are used most discriminately: spring cherry tree blossoms, yes; beds of flowering perennials, no.

Because the garden itself functions as a haven for contemplation and reflection on our existence within the world, a winding garden path is essential to the design.

A sense of mystery is evoked by the hidden scenes beyond the curves, and then a breathtaking surprise appears with the discovery of a waterfall, pond, or scene.

Details are critical—the choices of stone and their placement, and the plants themselves, selected with an eye for texture, tone, and form. Even the placement of décor, such as the traditional stone lantern, is dictated by its use, such as lighting a path for the evening walk to the teahouse, the lantern's opening facing the area it would illuminate.

Including a garden pond is

essential in the Japanese garden. While these ponds may include water lilies and water irises in the shallows, reflective open water surface is more typical. Natural streams and waterfalls are more characteristic than the inclusion of many aquatic plants. Color is often supplied by cherished Koi fish. Stepping stones across the clear water surface or a zigzag bridge mandating a leisurely stroll across the water invites observation and enjoyment of the Koi.

The essence of a Japanese garden recreates, in miniature, the arresting beauty found in nature. In Japan, mountain streams are sources of immense peace and tranquility. Judicious pruning of pines creates the illusion they are naturally affected by harsh mountain winds.

A Japanese garden makes use of traditional, well-pruned plantings, set aesthetically among rocks around the concrete pool.

Water Features for Every Garden

A stylized Japanese water-feature design by Larry Leone of Dallas, Texas, features unique stone combined with traditional black pebbles. At the top of the feature, Larry uses a bamboo spout and a smooth, handmade stone vessel to recycle the water.

A large-scale Japanese garden, set within the Sonnenburg Estate in Rochester, New York, displays the artful balance of space, plantings, water, and stone.

This water iris-lined stream is part of the Japanese garden at the Denver Botanic Garden. Stone and green plantings act as a foil to the brief burst of color in early summer from the purple irises.

Another Larry Leone design contrasts mounded streamside plantings with carefully placed stonework. Smooth river pebbles fill in between larger rocks to create the sense of wear by the flowing water.

Smooth black pebbles are often used in Japanese landscape design.

As in nature, the Japanese stream focuses on rock placements and their combinations.

Typical of mountain streams, elevation changes in small stair-steps are framed by larger rocks, often appearing as walls that have been cut through by the flowing water.

Even a narrow, trickling stream demands careful selection and individual placement of stones.

At the Denver Botanic Garden, you'll find another traditional Japanese design element: wooden posts set on end.

Mortared among smooth river pebbles, an arrangement of posts lends a Japanese design element next to the Koi pond.

An adaptation of wooden posts is found in this Pacific Coast garden. To prevent any sharp edges within the water from injuring the special Koi, the rubber liner is affixed to the posts above the water line.

Stone lanterns are often found in Japanese gardens where evening tea ceremonies require lighted pathways. Set the lantern so the candlelight will fall on the path or be reflected into the water nearby. This New York garden sites a lantern to shine upon what is actually a dry stream bed created with flat, black slate.

A pondside lantern is appropriately placed against a backdrop of pine needles and soft deciduous foliage.

An interesting placement of a Japanese stone lantern is upon a ledge within the pond itself.

Ah, bamboo! What Japanese garden is complete without it? Although many bamboos are perfectly hardy in cold climate zones, use caution when including it within your garden design. Its spread must be rigorously monitored, and it should not be planted anywhere near a lined pond or stream as bamboo will puncture a pond liner. On the other hand, bamboo planted along a natural lake is confined by the water. Bamboo is not an aquatic plant.

In this Larry Leone design, note the curving pathway and the illusion that more of the garden is hidden from view, waiting to surprise the garden visitor around the next bend. Note, too, the use of mounding plants in various shades of green. In selecting plants, if they do not normally grow in clean mound forms, choose plants that will accommodate such pruning. The gently arched bridge echoes the plant forms while the lantern, providing vertical interest to the design, hints that a special place for nighttime visitation exists beyond the bridge.

Because bridges and stepping stones are heavy themselves and will bear the weight of people on them, they must be strongly constructed. If you know where the bridge will be located before building your pond, install concrete support-slabs within the pond excavation before you fit in the liner. If you don't know in advance and the bridge will be constructed after the pond is installed, supply padding such as Styrofoam or pieces of scrap liner to protect your liner. If necessary, use a flat concrete slab to distribute the weight. The actual bridge or stepping stone is supported by posts or pedestals set within concrete-filled containers on the prepared site. For safety's sake, install stepping stones and bridges above the water level.

There is a reason for zigzag bridges and stepping stones in Japanese garden design: both invite slow, cautious movement. Safe crossing demands that you pause between each step. While you pause, why not look around? Watch the fish swim, enjoy the scent of a night-blooming water lily, or simply enjoy the views of the garden.

Deer scares are another decorative but functional element in the Japanese garden. These water features function from a hidden reservoir that feeds one bamboo tube that, when sufficiently weighted with water, tilts downward to flow the water into the second tube. Emptied of water, the tubes then return to position...with a distinct, loud, tapping sound meant to scare away deer. Because some people find the repetitive knocking sound irritating, deer scares are often used solely as decoration.

Water Features for Every Garden

CHAPTER THIRTEEN

The Evening Garden

Still open in the early morning hours, the fragrant night-blooming, tropical water lily N. 'Missouri' is spectacular at night.

Nightscaping Gardens and Ponds

TRADITIONALLY, an evening garden is a white garden, full of scented plants. Moonlight is captured in white petals and silver foliage as sweet or spicy scents fill the air. Light-colored stone highlights garden pathways, and white garden structures anchor surrounding plants.

For the larger pond, the night-blooming, tropical Victoria *offers both fragrance and pristine white, first-night flowers.*

Today, however, acknowledging that people often cannot spend daylight hours in their gardens, another design element characterizes the evening garden—lighting. Garden lighting includes aesthetics—uplighting, backlighting, and spotlighting garden plants and structures. It may merely illuminate the garden design, or it may create a totally different, fanciful garden. It also includes function—lighting pathways and entertainment areas and enhancing home security.

Nightscaping is the art of lighting the nighttime landscape. Most easily planned in advance to accommodate necessary wiring and installation, it can be accomplished in stages. Often the first stage is lighting the entertainment area, usually directly behind the home. This lighting should be bright enough for activities, yet adjustable to soft moods, too.

Other mood lighting, such as uplighting a tree, is done for effect. Path lighting provides illumination for elevation changes within the landscape, as well as guidance for safe transit in the garden.

The traditionally classic "white garden," as exemplified in the Sonnenberg Estate garden in New York, is designed for evening enjoyment.

Select plants with white-variegated foliage, white flowers, or white to silvery blue foliage for the evening garden. Plant these light-reflective plants next to garden paths.

Lighting dark areas of the garden can provide both effect and safety.

Garden lighting imitates nature with downlighting and backlighting effects. Imagine the moon shining down on the garden to guide downlighting placements. While visiting a home in Dallas, I was amazed by this concept. In spite of a night misted by rain, the entire garden seemed lit by moonlight. Lacy foliage patterned the ground below trees bearing lights carefully placed and hidden above. The effect was astounding. Backlighting is similar to the effect of the setting sun shining through plantings and producing silhouettes. Especially effective with structural plantings, backlighting creates a different vision of the daytime garden.

Other ways to create a different landscape at night are uplighting and crosslighting to produce shadows on background walls. Spotlighting special garden structures, such as statuary, arbors, or water-

The curved garden path is lighted where the path alters to keep both visitors and plantings safe from harm.

falls, changes the garden vision, too.

Most garden lighting is planned with low-voltage, 12-volt lighting systems that run through transformers. Transformers convert the 120-volt electricity used in the home to less expensive 12-volts. Transformers are rated in total watts, such as 100 watts or 250 watts. In planning the

lights to run off the transformer, add the wattage of all lights in the system to prevent the lights from dimming. The wattage run through the system should not exceed 80% of the capacity of the transformer.

Remember, too, that electricity is lost along the wiring the further it is from the transformer. Keep cable runs to less than one hundred feet for each circuit.

Low-voltage cable is specified in gauges and is sold as 12-2, 14-2, 16-2, etc. with the first number representing the gauge and the second indicating that it is a two-wire cable. With wire, the lower the gauge, the thicker the wire and the less loss of electricity over long runs. 12-gauge is most commonly used. If the system is equipped with a photocell timer, the lights automatically go on at dusk and shut off at dawn.

Mount the transformer on the outside of the house and run it through a waterproof ground-fault circuit inter-

The garden visited frequently in the evening should present safe pathways. If the pathway is not lit, keep it straight for safe movement.

Pinkie Marx, a watercolor artist in Missouri, discovered one year that her tiny white holiday lights were attractive enough to leave up year-round.

rupter (GFCI). If the lighting is installed before the garden is built, install one-inch conduits under solid features such as pavement. However, if the garden already exists, bore under existing paving to install the wiring conduits, or run the wires around the obstruction, increasing the length of the run and possibly limiting its function.

Select your fixtures and bulbs by their intended use. Path lights illuminate garden walkways and use a bayonet-

Safely constructed and lit, pathways allow garden enjoyment around the clock.

John Haylek collects circus and carnival memorabilia. His neon frog-on-a-lily-pad light is perfectly sited above a small water garden, providing lighthearted illumination to nighttime garden visits.

Attractive during the day, this garden fixture casts light across the tiered waterfall.

Attractive low-voltage garden lighting is available in many styles at home centers. Run through a transformer affixed with a ground-fault circuit interrupter, the lights can be set by timers, turning on at dusk and off at dawn.

style bulb. Tuck them among plantings along the path to avoid creating a runway effect. Bayonet style bulbs are also used to downlight from overhead trees. Although most kits come with 4- or 7-watt bulbs, downlighting is most effective with 11- to 20-watt bulbs.

Use spotlights to uplight, downlight, backlight, and highlight. Consider effect lighting. This can also light pathways if directed downward from a tree onto a path.

Par-36 bulbs, the same as car headlights, throw a beam a long way and are used to uplight trees. MR-16 bulbs are high-intensity, tungsten, halogen bulbs that give a truer white light and produce more accurate colors at night. Both of these bulbs are used within ground-canister units.

Specialty lights can be mounted into steps, walls, and deck railings for a variety of uses, including water applications. Few lighting effects

match the drama of illuminating water features. Most water garden supply centers offer revolving fountain lights and underwater lights. In deciding to use underwater lights, remember that any suspended particulates will seem to be magnified. Also, underwater lights should not be left on all night as they disrupt resting fish. Underwater low-voltage lights are especially effective set at the base of a waterfall entry, where they produce a dramatic glow to the moving water.

Other lighting options create dramatic nighttime effects with water displays. Light the surrounding landscape to highlight the water. Use spotlights with MR-16 bulbs to cast light across the stone work in the pond or across the waterfall to shadow the moving water on the rocks behind. Light a plant next to the pond to create reflections on the water. Shine a spotlight up a creek or on a night-blooming water lily.

Tiki torches provide enough light for entertaining in the garden. Votive candles softly light the pondside vignette.
Photo by Jim Lersch

Soft path lights lead visitors to a unique, satellite-dish gazebo. For quiet conversation, the bright gazebo lighting is extinguished in favor of magical white twinkling lights. Photo by Jim Lersch

When a pond is included in the entertainment area, path-lighting its edges enhances safety as well as aesthetics and mood. Photo by Jim Lersch

Tiki torches and low-voltage pathway lights keep the pondside entertainment area safe. Photo by Jim Lersch

Brighter lights near the house serve activity and security. Softer path lighting leads visitors safely into the nighttime garden. Photo by Jim Lersch

Mini porch lights display trolls' nightlife around the pond. An underwater light at the waterfall extends the magic. Photo by Jim Lersch

CHAPTER FOURTEEN

The Shady Garden

*Shady gardens are usually serenely green. Design elements of
wood and stone are more important than flowers.*

Waterfalls

THINK shady garden, and the woodland garden comes to mind. However, a shade garden can be of any garden style, the only requirement being shade produced by trees, shrubs, and structures. Plants are selected according to the particular garden design. The woodland garden, for example, displays native woodland plants. Winding natural paths lead the visitor to scene after serene scene, including a rocky stream and quiet pool. The Japanese garden celebrates nature—selections pay attention to plant forms and water. The cultivated shade garden, of course, is a hosta and fern haven. Generally, various shades of green livened with white, cream, and yellow variegations are the mainstay of the shady garden. Color can still be supplied, perhaps most notably with the season-long blooming impatiens.

A modestly blooming plant to include in the shallows of your pond or stream is Houttuynia. The colorful cordata or chameleon plant displays little color in shady conditions.

Because most blooming aquatic plants require sunny conditions, a shady water garden often acquires its color from colorful fish and from perimeter plantings of impatiens. The real joy of a shady pond is the pristine serenity of clear, sparkling water. Quiet reflections of gently arching edge plantings and flashes of color from goldfish or Koi add ambiance. The effect of floating water-lily leaves is attained with the planting of spatterdock or *Nuphar*. If the

A shady New York pond enjoys the bold presence of red-blooming impatiens with the subtle foil of white-blooming lizard tail (Saururus) in the pond. Shady conditions are especially appropriate for the Koi pond since Koi colors fade in direct sunlight.

When Craig Luna designs a shady garden in Atlanta, no corner is left without detail: variegated foliage in both ivies and the dwarf sweet flag planted directly within the stream, textured mosses, hostas, ferns, and impatiens for a splash of color.

pond has even two or three hours of sunlight exposure, a few hardy water lilies will still bloom: 'James Brydon,' 'Escarboucle,' and 'Attraction' are red selections; 'Chromatella' is yellow; 'Masaniello' is pink; and 'Hal Miller' is a large, creamy white. As for tropical water lilies, look to the blues for shade-tolerant blooms.

Often water features in the shady garden focus on the sight and sound of moving water–rocky streams or waterfalls. The only requirement to create a waterfall is a change in elevation. If the property is flat, soil from a pond excavation or trucked topsoil creates the elevation changes. Carve stair-steps into the mounded soil to construct a waterfall. The stair-steps may include as many elevation changes as desired; lovely falls are created with only a single change in elevation. Use a single piece of pond liner to fully line the excavation, bringing the edges well above the anticipated water level. Unlike pond construction, for this purpose the liner can be pieced, as long as

The focal point of this shady Louisiana garden is the water tumbling over huge boulders.

A shady garden becomes even more peaceful with the addition of a pond, flowing stream, and waterfall.

the piecing occurs at elevation changes where the overlap of upper over lower pieces is not submerged. The liner is eventually tucked into the surrounding soil and well hidden by rocks, soil, and plants. Water flow can be a smooth sheet flowing over a straight-edged, spillway rock, or it can be a frothy tumble over variously sized cobbles stacked or mortared into a slope. To finish off a waterfall, anchor it within its landscaped setting by extending rocks out into the surrounding area. Hide its water source around a curve or within plants and rocks to naturalize your construction. (See Chapter 17 for stream ideas.)

Want a splash of color with your shady garden stream? Craig Luna packed a bit of soil into the ends of a small hollow log and planted pink impatiens.

The shady garden is perfectly suited to a Koi pond. Lush greens in hostas, ferns, variegated sweet flag (Acorus calamus 'Variegata'), and a Japanese maple frame the crystal waters and colorful Koi.

Water, stone, and ferns—a most beautiful combination.

Friends have dubbed this Pennsylvania pond "the rainforest pond" for its lush plantings. Short on blooming plants, the garden nevertheless bears a wondrous collection of shade-tolerant and shade-loving plants.

With a limited choice of blooming plants for shady water gardens, experiment with variegated foliage plants to provide life and contrast.

The shade garden invites attention to texture and form. Large rocks create a waterfall, and the lacy-leaved Corydalis tucked among them contrasts further with the larger foliaged shrubs on the opposite side.

In the Japanese garden in Manato Public Park in Spokane, Washington, this waterfall combines two interesting water effects: a narrow sheeting fall and a lively cascade over a cobbled courseway.

The waterfall in this woodland garden began with a stair-step construction requiring an elevated mound, which was perfectly supplied by natural terrain.

This Ohio backyard slopes greatly from the house to its furthest perimeter. A three-foot drop from the back patio to the next level of the yard creates the setting for a charming shady water garden with a lush, ivy backdrop.

Water Features for Every Garden

A bio-filter at the top of the waterfall construction bears lips on opposite sides so that the water overflows into two separate waterfalls, each feeding separate parts of the water garden.

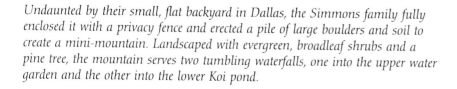

A fake-rock construction creates a unique, narrow waterfall that is fed from a small reservoir at its base.

Undaunted by their small, flat backyard in Dallas, the Simmons family fully enclosed it with a privacy fence and erected a pile of large boulders and soil to create a mini-mountain. Landscaped with evergreen, broadleaf shrubs and a pine tree, the mountain serves two tumbling waterfalls, one into the upper water garden and the other into the lower Koi pond.

You don't need a great change in elevation to create a waterfall. This waterfall connects an upper Koi pond through a stream to a lower Koi pond. Although the waterfall itself is less than a foot high, the pump selection considers the total difference in height from the back of the upper Koi pond (where the recycled water first enters the system) to the lowest elevation from where the water is pumped, along with the linear feet between the two sites. Generally, plan for 100 to 150 gallons per hour per inch of spillway and another 100 gallons per hour per 10 linear feet of distance between exit and entry points. Find the total elevation (or "head") on the pump manufacturer's chart and follow that column down to the amount of gallons per hour you need.

When constructing a stream or a waterfall near a tree, dealing with roots is a problem. Too much disturbance can injure the tree. Once the feature has been installed, continued root growth can penetrate the construction. Specially treated geothermal textile can be used to avert root intrusions.

Running out of space for more ponds, Ben and Kit Knotts resorted to a pond across the front of their Florida home, essentially creating a driveway pond. The lowest pond functions as a reservoir to feed the top overflowing pond with recycled water. Kit keeps the flow gentle to protect her incredible collection of tropical water lilies.

Water Features for Every Garden

CHAPTER FIFTEEN

The Marsh/Damp Garden

Marsh marigold, Caltha palustris, *is one of the early delights of spring in wet and marshy woodlands.*

Bog Gardens

OCCASIONALLY or perpetually wet areas of the garden need not be soggy, barren landscapes. While there are many plants that need constant moisture, finding the plants that do well in both extremes of dry and wet is more complicated. In planning to landscape such a difficult area, first look to your native plants. Explore the countryside for wet-to-dry stream beds, river banks of fluctuating waters, and low-lying areas that flood in spring but remain dry all summer. In your explorations, you may find certain aquatic plants that do well under the extreme conditions of wet to dry and back: cattails, rushes, and water irises, for example.

Only two landscape timbers deep, this marsh garden is set within a flowerbed.

Spend time with favorite garden books for suggestions of plants adaptable to such changing conditions, too. If you are uncertain whether a plant can tolerate the extremes, check with local nurseries or your county extension office. One of the most useful terrestrial plants to include is the daylily (*Hemerocallis*). Quite by accident, I discovered one year that daylilies, known to survive drought conditions well, could just as easily live in fully wet conditions year-round.

Actually planning a freshwater marsh garden may be a desirable aspect of your gardenscape. Likewise, you may decide that a true bog garden, typically of peaty soil and a haven for acid-loving, moisture-loving plants, is your desire. Both of these gardens can be created within the backyard garden, in much the same manner as installing a pond.

To create a marsh, damp, or bog garden, excavate as though for a shallow pond of 18 to 24 inches. Line the excavation with pond liner. This design is a good use for scrap pieces of pond liner as some

This collection of shallow water aquatic plants at Longwood Garden displays the broad selection available.

soaker hose within the top of the excavation. Return the excavated soil to the feature and enhance it as necessary. True bog plants, for example, need acidic soil, mandating the addition of copious amounts of peat. A freshwater bog needs only heavy topsoil.

Since the damp garden remains uniformly wet, use flat stepping stones to ease garden maintenance. A thick layer of mulch helps retain moisture in the soil. While selections can be planted directly into the wet bed, keeping them within large, holeless containers prevents rampant spread and compli-cated maintenance. Any shallow-water aquatic plant can be grown in a marsh/damp garden. An alternative method is not to return the soil to the lined excavation, keeping the garden merely as a shallow pond only 12 to 18 inches deep. Even dwarf or pygmy water lilies can be included in such marsh ponds.

seepage or drainage prevents the damp garden from becoming rank. If you use a single piece of liner, perforate it throughout to allow slow drainage.

Cover the liner with a layer of several inches of stone. To include a source for replen-ishing the water supply, bury a

If only one species is grown within the marsh garden, the shallow pond can be half-filled with soil and the plants set directly into the soil. This method creates problems if several species are grown together; vigorously growing aquatic plants do need thinning and division.

Pitcher plants and other carnivorous plants appreciate acidic soil and adequate moisture.

Steve Stroupe has created numerous shallow-water ponds for growing lotuses around his home. One of them uses a preformed pond unit that is comouflaged by Steve's carpentry talents. Inside the pond is an acidic soil suitable for the moisture-loving Nepenthe, the carnivorous pitcher plant.

Commonly called "bog gardens" to indicate their lack of depth, most of the plants grown in these gardens are, in fact, freshwater marsh plants. Although they are so lushly planted as to deny visibility of the water, there are, in fact, two or three inches of water over the tops of the potted plants in the bogs next to this gazebo.

Water irises are particularly suited to shallow-water plantings around a pond. The Louisiana Iris family offers the greatest variety in flower form and color.

Whiskey-barrel-size containers display collections of marginal aquatic plants. Centered near the fence, three tubs set within and upon the ground grow variegated rushes, cattails, and water irises. To the right, three more barrels are set within the ground of a raised flowerbed to display lotuses.

By constructing a shallow shelf in the pond excavation and then enclosing it with a water-permeable divider, a marsh garden is created. This marsh garden is separated from the pond with wood.

A shallow water garden, no more than 12 inches deep, displays attractive marginal aquatics and even a dwarf water lily.

A swimming pool converted to a water garden includes a shallow bog area. Water recycled from the pond enters the rear of the shallow planting area and flows through it, allowing vegetable filtration to help keep the pond water clear.

Ideas for our own gardens abound in public botanical gardens. At Missouri Botanical Garden, the large Japanese garden's pond features a wooden-framed garden set within the pond to display the early summer blooms of water irises.

A shallow shelf construction can also be framed with rocks to create interesting plant and rock combinations along the edge of the pond. If the rocks are set closely enough together, the planting pocket can be filled with soil, and plants can be grown directly in it.

At the opposite end of Chuck Thomas's bog garden, a mini-bog was created with the soil enhanced with peat to create conditions to grow pitcher plants.

Taro, Esculenta sp. *is often grown in the terrestrial garden. Water gardeners, of course, know this plant family as a lush pond plant. One way to keep these plants perfectly happy out in the terrestrial garden is to plant them within a concealed bog garden-- lined and kept mulched to retain moisture.*

A bog garden need not have clearly defined borders nor a visible level of water. Chuck Thomas in Birmingham, Alabama, designed this bog garden with a pond liner to keep the water within the area of the garden. This section of his bog garden displays lotuses, water irises, and white rushes (Scirpus albescens) amid a lush "ground covering" of parrot's feather.

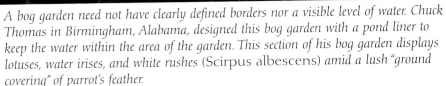

CHAPTER SIXTEEN

The Vignette Garden

A vignette of a child fishing off the end of the dock, his rowboat tied up nearby, evokes fond childhood memories.

Flowing Water

WITH modern lifestyles turning us to recreation and relaxation within our own backyards, we decorate those outdoor living areas, just as we decorate the inside of our homes. Why not include angels in our gardens if we collect and display them in the home? Why not recycle discardable family items like an old tricycle, an old wheelbarrow, a push lawnmower, baskets, garden shoes, whatever? Recycling these items and using crafts within the garden puts our individual stamp on the garden. Just as our homes reflect our personalities and lifestyle, so does the backyard garden.

Variegated ivy grows in a small jar held by a monkey, poised on the pond edge and framed by lizard tail (Saururus cernuus).

In decorating our gardens, we create vignettes—little scenes displaying crafts and garden décor. The garden pond naturally becomes part of the vignette: fairy, angel, and frog statues posing next to the pond and on waterfall ledges, a train track and miniature train traveling around the garden pond and through miniature landscape scenes; or a miniature boat tied up to the edge of the pond. Vignettes can be natural, too, with artful arrangements of driftwood, special stones, and mosses. The vignette garden most expresses our individual personalities and lifestyles. It offers the same options as decorating indoors—floors, walls, ceilings, and accessories—and like our homes, it includes plumbing. There are no limits.

Flowing water increases the decorating possibilities. Small flowing features can be part of vignettes, too: a spitting frog perched on a bench to recycle water from a container garden below; a tiered design flowing water from the basin reservoir to the top where it spills one into the other until it returns to the

Elusive live frogs are part of many water gardens. Frog statuary, however, creates ever-present vignettes of favorite amphibians.

Childhood is a time of simple pleasures, evoked here by special garden statuary.

basin below; endless possibilities of plumbed statuary and items—the only requirements being that the basin-reservoir be watertight and tubing connect the submersible pump to its flow partner.

Small pumps in the 80-to-300 GPH range use narrow plastic tubing attached to the pump and to the statue's outlet. Using black tubing alleviates the accumulation of algae and the slowing of the flow of water.

A heron statue, although supposedly a deterrent to live herons, functions solely as decoration during heron breeding and nesting season.

Beside creating miniature villages and scenes along the pond's railroad track, a clear plastic tunnel protects the train in this waterfall scene.

If the truth be known, railroad ponds are the obsessive dream of many grown-up pond owners!

Create a miniature seaside fishing village on the edge of your pond.

A simple piece of driftwood, Japanese-style posts, moss-covered rocks, and a trickling stream create a natural vignette in a shady stream.

Using driftwood as part of the in-pond vignette is more than an aesthetic creation--it invites birds to be part of the living scene.

A vignette can be as simple as an elegant vessel. Antique-finished reproductions are available at fine garden centers.

A plumbed, cherubic statue becomes the focal point of the water garden when posed atop the waterfall.

Create a vignette with a plumbed statue by framing it with plants and giving it an undistracting background.

A small raised pond displays a plumbed statue.

An overflowing vessel set within a sunny pond acquires a natural algae coating that ages the feature.

Plumbed statuary creates charming vignettes when set within the pond water.

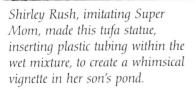

Classic statuary, set within the pond amidst fowering ornamental grasses, creates an elegant vignette

Shirley Rush, imitating Super Mom, made this tufa statue, inserting plastic tubing within the wet mixture, to create a whimsical vignette in her son's pond.

Small plumbed statues are commonly called "spitters." Combining a group of statuary around the plumbed figure creates a charming vignette on the edge of the pond.

A working water wheel and mill house create a scene of long ago. The mill house serves a dual purpose by housing pond supplies and out-of-pond filtration and pumps.

Vary the effect of water pouring from a small bucket or barrel by setting a "mister" within the bucket. Be sure the sides of your bucket extend high enough above the water level to contain splashes.

Linda Siler created a unique in-pond flowing feature with a tall stack of blocks that she plumbed to flow water from its top. A classic lion's head and surrounding aquatic plants complete the scene.

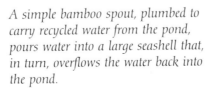

A simple bamboo spout, plumbed to carry recycled water from the pond, pours water into a large seashell that, in turn, overflows the water back into the pond.

An Asian accent to a recycling "waterfall" uses a tee connection behind the water feature to split the water flowing from the submerged pump into four tubes that fit inside the bamboo pipes.

Drill a hole in the bottom of an earthenware vessel and paint the inside with a sealant to prevent weeping and algae-coating. Tilt the vessel on its side so that the water plumbed in through the bottom flows naturally back into the pond.

If a stronger flow is desired for a different look, increase the size of the pump.

Drilling holes through rocks is not the quickest of tasks, but it can be done. Stack the rocks in the center of a pond, plumbing them from a submerged pump below, and create a flowing vignette.

Two classic garden features, a hand pump and a wheelbarrow, cascade water back into the pond in the test gardens at Southern Living magazine, in Birmingham.

To make a flowing-water feature, connect tubing to the submerged pump's outtake and direct it to the partner vessel. In this flowing watering can, the tubing is enclosed within a metal tube that is soldered into the bottom of the can.

A favorite Asian vessel is plumbed and fitted with a bell fountain head.

Pinkie Marx wanted an overflowing fountain within her swimming pool. She used one of the water-return jets from the pool to supply the fountain via a clear plastic tube.

CHAPTER SEVENTEEN

The Stream Garden

Streams bring the element of water out into the garden.

Streams

A REAL *bird attracter, the stream garden graces your landscape with flowing water. The stream can be wide or narrow, straight or curved, deep enough to run smoothly, or shallow and cobbled to provide ripples and eddies in its journey.*

The stream garden is compatible with any garden style. Make it natural-looking and tuck it amid rocks and plants. Let it roam through a sunny green expanse or flower bed, or let it meander among shade-loving ferns and hostas in a woodland setting. Give it varying levels with small cascades to liven its path. Make it formal with a brick-lined courseway. Whatever your scheme, you need only provide a source of its water.

Side pockets set within the camouflaged liner bed of the stream allow growing marginal aquatic plants that naturalize the feature. Parrot's feather, producing a lush accent to the stream, is simply tucked among the rocks. Note also the use of flat base stones to provide slight elevation drops to the stream, as well as the placement of larger stones within the stream bed.

The head waters for this stream construction are concealed back among dense foliage to make the stream appear natural.

Water Features for Every Garden

Often the water source for a stream is a garden pond with the water cycled from the pond to the head of the stream, from there flowing through the course to return to the pond/reservoir. The biggest concern with this construction is that the amount of water involved in the stream not be so significant as to noticeably drop the water level in the pond when the stream is in operation. Likewise, you don't want the pond to flood when the stream is shut off and its water pours back into the pond. Figure the volume of the stream by computing length x width x depth in feet. Since most streams run shallow, you can use an average figure for a three-inch depth such as 0.25, or a quarter of a foot. Once you know the estimated volume of water involved in your stream construction, you can look at its reservoir pond to determine the effect of removal of that amount of water. An 8 x 10-foot pond, for example, will drop about three-quarters of an inch in servicing a 10-foot-long stream. The same pond, however, in servicing a 25-foot-

This slow-moving stream runs the entire length of the backyard and is set amid bird- and butterfly-attractive plants.

long stream, will drop nearly two inches. (A square foot of water one inch deep holds .083 gallons of water.) To service your stream from a hidden, in-ground reservoir, plan for your reservoir to hold 2.5 times the total volume involved in the stream. Initially, monitor the water level in the reservoir to determine the average rate of evaporation from your stream and the required frequency of topping-off the reservoir.

Generally, the head of a stream is higher in elevation than its reservoir, although this elevation need be no greater than one inch per ten linear feet. Mark the ground for your excavation much as you would for a pond installation. Make your elevation wide and deep enough to accommodate whatever rocks will line it.

Design elements of curves and drops in elevation make for interest in the stream, as well as creating the illusion that the stream is longer than perhaps it really is. Likewise, create the head of the stream's source to make it seem its source is further away. The stream can begin, for example, emerging from landscape foliage or from an arrangement of rocks.

A natural stream design uses smaller rocks within the stream bed with larger rocks along the edge. Singularly placed larger rocks within the stream bed provide further design interest as well as variation in the water flow.

Line the stream with a watertight membrane. Piecing the liner can cause seepage and water loss, as it can in a pond.

Emerging from a hidden source among foliage at the back of the property, this Pennsylvania stream separates the lawn from a planted, shady bed. With the stream liner dipping back down into the surrounding soil and the edging rocks hiding it, it's possible for grass to be brought up to the edge of the stream. Water forget-me-nots grow happily in the slow-moving water.

Take advantage of a natural drainage ditch and turn it into a stream garden.

It is possible, however, to piece a stream liner if the liner overlaps only at points of elevation change, the pieced portion not being submerged and the top overlapping the lower-level liner. Extend the liner beyond the stream bed with enough extra to allow it to be brought up above the projected water level and concealed in the surrounding landscape.

Once the liner is in place, begin building the stream. Start from the outer edges and work across. Mortar the rocks in place on the liner to prevent water from flowing beneath them and to ensure a flowing display over the rocky base. Mark elevation changes with small cascades over a smooth-edged spillway or over cobbled sections of the channel, much like a mountain stream. Select smooth, rounded cobbles for the stream bed to create a natural look. Craggier rocks can be used in the perimeter. Lining your stream bed with very small stones or sand does not usually work as the flowing water carries them downstream to form dams. However, a pebble base is easily

This shady stream has Craig Luna's name written all over it: details, details, details, in both the surrounding landscape and within the stream itself.

Selecting plants to edge your stream presents a problem of finding plants that appear naturally to love the moister conditions yet can grow in the normal garden conditions that exist on the other side of the pond liner used in the water feature. This pond design makes use of Ajuga, which appreciates moist conditions but which tolerates normal garden conditions. Where the plant has spread into the stream bed, happiness abounds.

mortared into place to create the illusion.

After the stream is completed, begin the water flow and make final decisions about rock placements. If the stream cycles from a pond stocked with fish, run enough water through the system to prevent leaching lime from harming the fish.

Set within a raised bed, a narrow stream is the focal point of the landscape plantings.

Curving the stream through the landscape creates the illusion of length and evokes a sense of mystery. What lies around the bend? Note the use of native stone along the edge of this Missouri pond and the similarly colored pea gravel.

Botanical gardens offer examples and ideas to translate into your own garden. This stream in the Missouri Botanical Garden's Japanese garden is made from a concrete-formed base and then naturalized with rocks and plantings. Note the winding path of the stream and the rippling water created by rocks lining the stream bed.

A cottage garden stream makes extensive use of flowering annuals, along with succession-blooming perennials, all brought up to the edge of the flowing stream. Water hyacinths are anchored within the stream bed by rocks set on their long, trailing roots.

This winding stream connects a Koi pond off the back deck to a water garden away from the house. With lawn on one side of the stream, the other side is landscaped with low-maintenance Sedum 'John Creech.' Smoothly rounded river rocks in the edging are echoed in the river-smoothed cobbles and pea gravel in the stream bed.

A narrow stream winds gently down the sloped perimeter of this Minnesota property. Rocks invite birds to bathe and drink from the stream.

A planted stream used with a water garden supplies natural vegetable filtration to help keep the pond water clear. One of the best plants to grow in moving water is watercress, Nasturtium officinale.

Marginal aquatic plants that grow in water with their growth emerging above the water level are good candidates for in-stream planting. Regular garden cannas appreciate these wet growing conditions.

Japanese dwarf sweet flag (Acorus gramineus) is one aquatic that can be planted directly within a stream bed since its growth tends to develop in tight clumps.

A xeriscaped, raised rock garden includes a stream that begins at the top of the mound and winds around through the rocks to a pond at ground level.

Birds readily accept the invitation to enjoy your garden stream if your edging rocks allow them access. A piece of driftwood adorning the stream gives the birds a place to preen after their splash baths. Note the tropical umbrella palm (Cyperus alternifolius) enjoying a summer outside, tucked within the stream bed.

Water Features for Every Garden

CHAPTER EIGHTEEN

The Room-After-Room/ Private Garden

The garden entry, a bridge, invites the garden visitor to explore the many rooms included in the outdoor living area.

Garden Bridges and Entries

*D*URING *the Italian Renaissance, the wealthy celebrated the garden as an outdoor living room. Today we see a renaissance in garden design, again returning to claim our gardens as family living space. Yet, this modern renaissance is not confined to the wealthy; even the smallest garden of the most modest home can be part of the family living space.*

Part of the fun of designing an outdoor living space is dividing the garden into separate areas by function: a children's play area, an entertainment area, a private relaxation area, and whatever other areas reflect the family's interests and lifestyle. The Rickard family in Ohio, for example, explain their garden design as "room-after-room." Immediately out the back door and tucked into the sheltered patio is a large Koi pond. Comfortable chairs and tables invite enjoyment of the

Even an open backyard can be divided into interest areas to create the feeling of room-after-room within the garden.

Within the outdoor living area, an arbor forms the entry to another garden room.

pet fish even during rain. Leaving the patio area, an arbor and bridge announce the entry into another "room." There, a lushly planted water garden is the center of a paved relaxation area. The pond is fed by a stream emerging from Rose of Sharon and butterfly bushes. Running the length of the yard along the fence, the stream divides the open "game area" of the yard from the bird and butterfly garden. At the back of the garden, a waterfall and more bird and butterfly plantings create yet another "room." Tucked at the back of the open game area, a gazebo framed by marsh gardens creates a private entertainment area.

In the South, room-after-room gardens are created with garden walls that invite decorative treatments— tumbling vines, espaliered plants, garden plaques, and wall fountains.

Generally, the area closest to the home is kept as an entertainment area to allow access to the family kitchen. Even so, another room off in the garden can easily house a barbeque pit and dining area.

Pathways lead to the next garden room. Often the paths lead to the focal point.

Open-work pergolas, adorned with climbing plants, create secret, private areas within the garden. This pergola sits before a water garden where the garden visitor can enjoy its peace and tranquility protected from sunlight above.

A shrouded gate conceals the wonders of the inner garden, creating a sense of mystery.

A cozy courtyard garden that includes a small pond is discovered after passing through double antique columns "rescued" from the demolition of a circa-1900 home.

If a children's play area is included in the garden design, it is usually planned where it can be visible from the house. Often the various "rooms" are designed in favorite garden styles—a rose garden, a cutting garden, an herb garden, a shade garden, a mini-orchard, a vegetable garden, a water garden, or a private, secret garden. Considered a never-ending work in progress, the room-after-room style can be developed a season at a time. Create room divisions with screening plants and/or fences and walls.

Besides the garden's dividing walls, well-planned pathways lead the visitor through the garden. Entries to the individual areas are important and clue the visitor as to what magic lies in the next room. A cutting, wildlife, or cottage garden room, for example, invites entry with a rose- or clematis-draped arbor entry. A secret water garden gains both privacy and safety with a locked gate around its area. Bridges over dry or real running streams mark divisions of rooms, just as garden structures such as gazebos or pergolas identify the use of the area.

Probably the greatest attraction of designing a room-after-room garden is the fact that you can truly have it all. Instead of confining your garden design to one particular style complementary to your home, you can have a room for every style you like.

A small garden room, tucked into lush foliage, becomes a secret garden with a secret pond.

A bridge leads from the entertainment area into the open lawn area. Two preformed ponds are set on each side of the bridge to create the illusion of a large pond to be crossed in entering the next living area.

Combining a stone wall and a rustic pergola creates a real "secret garden" room.

Another version of the wooden plank bridge uses crosswise planks affixed to a gently arched foundation.

In selecting a bridge for your garden, keep its structure within perspective of the rest of the garden. Railings on the bridge provide a measure of safety.

A stone slab can be used as a low-profile bridge over a narrow expanse. If you use more than one slab with bridge supports existing within the water feature, provide adequate support and liner protection. (See Chapter 12.)

Bridges should be compatible with the home and landscape design. They should be used where they would be practical, even if they are not actually used.

A wooden plank bridge is easy to make for the informally styled garden. Make sure the bridge extends enough beyond the edge of the water feature to be securely anchored.

This gently arched plank bridge gains added design-interest with a decorative strip added to each side.

A multi-level garden with a gazebo at the very top adds safety railings to the plank bridge that are within proportion to the total garden.

Index

Converting to Metric

To convert	Multiply by	To obtain
inches	2.54	centimeters
inches	25.4	millimeters
feet	30	centimeters
pounds	0.45	kilograms
U.S. gallons	3.8	liters

Fahrenheit to Celsius: Subtract 32, multiply by 5, divide by 9